TRANSITION TO GREATER

by

'Lanre Somorin M.D.

Little Rock

2020

Unless otherwise noted, all scripture is from the King James Version of the Bible.

Scripture quotations marked AMPC are from The Amplified Bible, Old Testament ©1965,1987 by the Zondervan Corporation. The Amplified New Testament© 1958,1987 by The Lockman Foundation,

Scripture quotations marked MSG are from The Message. Copyright ©1993, 1995 by Eugene H. Peterson. Used by permission of NavPress Publishing Group

Scripture quotations marked NIV are from The Holy Bible, New International Version © 1973, 1978, 1984 by the International Bible Society. Used by permission of Zondervan Publishing House.

Scripture quotations marked NKJV Version are from the New King James Version © 1982 by Thomas Nelson Inc.

Transition to Greater

Copyright 2020 by 'Lanre Somorin, M.D.

Published by Faith 2 Fe Publishing Company
Little Rock, Arkansas 72205
Printed in the United States of America

ISBN-13: 978-1-949934-33-5

Printed in the United States of America. All rights reserved under International Copyright Law. No part of this publication may be reproduced, stored in a retrieval system or transmitted in any form or by any means-electronic, mechanical, photocopy, recording or any other- except for brief quotations in printed reviews, without the prior written permission of the author.

CONTENTS

DEDICATION V
INTRODUCTION VII
1. POSSESSING YOUR PROMISED LAND 1
2. DON'T UNPACK TOO EARLY 9
3. NECESSARY PREPARATIONS 21
4. LIVE LOADED 29
5. TAKE THE NEXT STEPS 43
6. SURMOUNTABLE OPPORTUNITIES 49
7. BREAKTHROUGH IN THE MIDST OF ADVERSITY ... 61

DEDICATION

I am delighted to dedicate this book to my lovely wife, Sade, and to our two wonderful children, Tobi and Tami.

To Sade, thanks for the support, encouragement, and the sweetness you add to my life. You are my best friend. Thanks for encouraging me to become an author.

To Tobi, for being such a wonderful son. Your drive for excellence is truly inspiring. It brings me a huge amount of joy to see what a fine young man you have become.

To Tami, my loving and affectionate daughter, who always looks out for her dad.

DEDICATION

INTRODUCTION

God never designed for us to be static. No matter where we are in our relationship with God, He always has more in store for us. Whether you don't know God or you already have a relationship with Him, He always wants to take you to greater heights.

PROVERBS 4:18 NKJV

18 But the path of the just is like the shining sun, That shines ever brighter unto the perfect day.

Your light is to be increasing in intensity until the perfect day.

EPHESIANS 3:20 NKJV

20 Now to Him who is able to do exceedingly abundantly above all that we ask or think, according to the power that works in us,

God is able to do much more than we can think or imagine. However, there is a limit to what God can do in our lives based on what we are doing right now. We often say we are waiting on God, but God requires us to position ourselves if we are going to experience greater in God. He is waiting for us to get into position. This book is designed to help you cooperate with that which you are sensing of God in your heart, that new direction, that new venture, new ministry, or expansion of something you already are doing. As you read this book, my prayer is that you will receive the tools to equip you to move from where you are to that place of greater and better. This could be in your relationship, your ministry, your career, finances or your vocation

Brace for increase!

Chapter One

Possessing Your Promised Land

THIS IS THE TIME FOR GROWTH. God has a position for us, and we must be in that position if we are going to experience victory. He has a specific location for us, which may include a geographical area or refer to a mental attitude. You may have to change your mindset to reach it. God gives victory, but the strategy and location are required to experience God's blessings.

When we talk about "transitioning to greater," we are speaking of a change that repositions us. A *transition* is "an act of faith in response to God's plan." We must be ready to move into position for all that God has in store for us. To enter the Promised Land, we must advance with confidence that the Lord has a plan and a provision.

We can't say, "God, You bring it closer because I am too afraid." Many times, we are located at Position "A," and the breakthrough is at Position "C." But we have to go through the road called "B" to reach our destination, and we don't like the challenges on the way. We could stay at Position "A" and pray and fast all that we want. But if God says it is over in a specific direction, we have to get up and move in that direction to take possession of the promise.

God's responsibility is the victory; our responsibility is to position

TRANSITION TO GREATER

ourselves. Opportunity comes when we are connected to a particular location. God told Jehoshaphat to position himself and his army, stand still and see the salvation of the Lord (2 Chron. 20:1–20).

2 CHRONICLES 20:1–3

1 It came to pass after this also, that the children of Moab, and the children of Ammon, and with them other beside the Ammonites, came against Jehoshaphat to battle.

2 Then there came some that told Jehoshaphat, saying, There cometh a great multitude against thee from beyond the sea on this side Syria; and, behold, they be in Hazazontamar, which is Engedi.

3 And Jehoshaphat feared, and set himself to seek the Lord, and proclaimed a fast throughout all Judah.

※ ※ ※

2 CHRONICLES 20:14-20

14 Then upon Jahaziel the son of Zechariah, the son of Benaiah, the son of Jeiel, the son of Mattaniah, a Levite of the sons of Asaph, came the Spirit of the Lord in the midst of the congregation;

15 And he said, Hearken ye, all Judah, and ye inhabitants of Jerusalem, and thou king Jehoshaphat, Thus saith the Lord unto you, Be not afraid nor dismayed by reason of this great multitude; for the battle is not yours, but God's.

16 Tomorrow go ye down against them: behold, they come up by the cliff of Ziz; and ye shall find them at the end of the brook, before the wilderness of Jeruel.

17 Ye shall not need to fight in this battle: set yourselves, stand ye still, and see the salvation of the Lord with you, O

> Judah and Jerusalem: fear not, nor be dismayed; tomorrow go out against them: for the Lord will be with you.
>
> **18** And Jehoshaphat bowed his head with his face to the ground: and all Judah and the inhabitants of Jerusalem fell before the Lord, worshipping the Lord.
>
> **19** And the Levites, of the children of the Kohathites, and of the children of the Korahites, stood up to praise the Lord God of Israel with a loud voice on high.
>
> **20** And they rose early in the morning, and went forth into the wilderness of Tekoa: and as they went forth, Jehoshaphat stood and said, Hear me, O Judah, and ye inhabitants of Jerusalem; Believe in the Lord your God, so shall ye be established; believe his prophets, so shall ye prosper.

The Word of God can become a revelation to us through study or speak prophetically to us as the man or woman of God ministers. In whatever manner it comes, the important thing is to receive and respond to the Word of God.

God doesn't change our destination. Instead, He puts us on the right road. When we are on the right path, we will arrive at the right destination. What many of us prefer is to stay where we are! The wrong road never becomes the right road just because we have been traveling on it for a long time. Some people think that, because they have been doing the same things over and over, eventually, God will have mercy on them and move them to their promised destination. No! We must be on the right road to arrive at the right destination.

If you are not on the right road, you can move over to the right one. If you are on the right road, then you need patience. If you have patience on the wrong path, that is a double whammy. You are out of luck! Having patience on the wrong road just prolongs your torture. You need to exit off the wrong road and get on the right one.

The inhabitants of Judah were surrounded by several armies. They called on the Lord, and He responded with a great victory. God's responsibility was the victory; the responsibility of the people was to be in the correct position.

What do you do when you are at one location, but your breakthrough is located at another? In the Bible, many people had to transition to obtain their breakthrough. To enter God's plan, Abraham had to change locations (Gen. 12:1-3). The prodigal son had to move out of the pigpen and return to his father's house (Luke 15:18). The three lepers had to leave their position by the gate (2 Kgs. 7:3). Even Joshua had to arise and position the people to cross the Jordan after the death of Moses (Josh. 1:2).

God does not change the location of your Promised Land to accommodate your fears and insecurities. It is called "a land" because it doesn't move. You must be the one to move if you are going to possess it. In my first book, *Seize Your Moment: Unmasking Everyday Opportunities,* I explain that opportunity comes when you are connected to a particular location. God said to the people of Judah, "Position yourselves."

My question to you is: What change in your position is God requiring? What transition is necessary to place you and your breakthrough in the same place at the same time? There is a location for the victory, and there is positioning for it.

GROWING INTO TRANSITION

The Lord expects us to grow up to possess the Promised Land, no matter how long that process takes. For the children of Israel, it took 40 years. The previous generation had to die out so God could raise another.

Don't walk past your Promised Land because you don't like the entrance. For example, you may be praying about a particular situation. God says, "This is what you need to do."

But you respond, "Oh, no! I don't like the giants in this Promised Land."

Regardless of the place God has told you to occupy, there may be some tenants, some giants inhabiting that place who have to be moved. That is why you must have a warrior mentality. Draw some boundaries around what belongs to you. Draw lines around your family, around your mind, and around your business.

God begins to increase your territory. For God to enlarge it, you need to identify your territory. Your Promised Land does not change over time; you need to move into it.

Many people stay in their wilderness, believing it will become the Promised Land. They pray and beg the Lord, saying, "God, help me." They are believing God, fasting, and trusting that, if they pray long enough, their current location will eventually become the Promised Land.

A This-and That Mentality

A hindrance occurs when we limit God to being a "consecutive-kind-of-God." What do I mean by that? *Consecutive* means "one step after the next, after the next." Sometimes in the vision or plan we have for our lives, we anticipate God has to do a certain thing first for the next thing to happen.

Perhaps you are in a particular position, for example, level eight.

TRANSITION TO GREATER

You believe that God will help you move to level nine and level ten. You think of all the dynamics that need to change for you to move into the next level. You consider the other people involved and what has to take place in their lives for you to change positions. If everything comes together, you should be able to move into level eleven. In a few years, if you play your cards right, you should advance to level twelve.

God is not a consecutive God. God is a simultaneous God, able to do more than one thing at the same time. God can give you a spouse, get you out of debt, pay off your mortgage, and move you into a new place all at the same time! It doesn't have to be sequential; it can be simultaneous—everything happening at the same time! You must be prepared to do more than one thing at the same time.

Often, I ask the Lord, "God, please tell me, is it *this* or *that?*"

God will usually say, "It is this and that." Begin to have a "This and That" mentality.

One example I can use from the technological advances of our society to illustrate this spiritual truth is the concept of direct deposit. I thank God for direct deposit! Set aside the idea that deposits can only be placed in your account every other Friday or once a month. Renew your mind of that limited thought process. You need to have multiple sources of income so that provision is hitting that account daily.

Sometimes, I check my account and boom! I see a deposit from Amazon, from the book sales. I think, *Oh, wow! Glory to God! That is another stream of income.*

You need to lift your expectations and say, "God, I am opening myself for You to be able to do more than one thing at a time." Everything can happen at the same time. Hallelujah!

He is a God of exceedingly, abundantly, above all we ask or think.

God is the One Who knows where that Land of Promise is located. God gave it to the Israelites, and then said, "You need to position yourselves." He gave them a strategy. "Stand still, and you will see the salvation of the Lord. Tomorrow, go out against them, for the Lord is with you (2 Chron. 20:17)."

BE CONVINCED OF THE VICTORY

Some people are not in the strategy phase because they haven't been convinced of the victory. They don't even believe! If they had not believed the prophet of the Lord, they would have never moved into the process of devising a plan.

We need to believe the Word of God! Whether it comes through the prophet, the pastor, or through the written Word of God, we must believe it. Then, we will get the strategy.

The Israelites could have said, "This doesn't make sense. This is very uplifting, but it makes no sense. Why should I position myself like this? Let's get more people to go and fight." God gave them the victory, but they had to be willing to flow with the strategy.

God always moved people into place to possess the land. He never moved the land to where they were. Many people are just waiting for God to bring the land to them.

PROVERBS 16:1

1 The preparations of the heart in man, and the answer of the tongue, is from the Lord.

The preparation and positioning belong to man. Preparation is our responsibility. In other words, the Lord is saying, "The victory is already won. You just have to prepare for it. You have to position

TRANSITION TO GREATER

yourself for it. Breakthrough is going to happen, and this is the strategy. You must flow with that strategy."

Chapter Two

Don't Unpack Too Early

THE DESTINATION WAS THE LAND OF CANAAN. The original plan was for them to go to the Promised Land. But they came to Haran and dwelt there. God has a location for your blessing. Until you get to that location, don't unpack.

> **GENESIS 12:1-4:**
>
> 1 Now the LORD had said unto Abram, Get thee out of thy country, and from thy kindred, and from thy father's house, unto a land that I will shew thee:
>
> 2 And I will make of thee a great nation, and I will bless thee, and make thy name great; and thou shalt be a blessing:
>
> 3 And I will bless them that bless thee, and curse him that curseth thee: and in thee shall all families of the earth be blessed.
>
> 4 So Abram departed, as the LORD had spoken unto him; and Lot went with him: and Abram was seventy and five years old when he departed out of Haran.

✳ ✳ ✳

TRANSITION TO GREATER
GENESIS 11:31

> 31 And Terah took Abram his son, and Lot the son of Haran his son's son, and Sarai his daughter in law, his son Abram's wife; and they went forth with them from Ur of the Chaldees, to go into the land of Canaan; and they came unto Haran, and dwelt there.

Terah planned to head to Canaan, but perhaps he reached Haran and thought, *You know what? I am not in Canaan yet. I know that is where I am meant to go, but at least Haran is better than the place from which I came. Let me just stay here. People around me won't know the difference. They know that it is better than where I came from, but they don't see the vision God gave me to go to Canaan.* He saw that Haran was better than where he came from and unpacked.

Do not unpack! If you have already unpacked, it is time to repack. We are heading to Canaan! Haran was a rest stop for them to refuel, get a phone charger, text a few people, update their social media, take some photos at the rest stop to let people know they were on their way, post on Instagram, and continue going toward Canaan.

Terah arrived in Haran. Perhaps he looked around and thought, *Oh, wow! Property is cheap around here. I could barely afford to live in Ur; why don't we just camp here? What's wrong with it?*

The Bible says his goal was to go to Canaan. He stopped in Haran, and something in Haran was attractive to him. It was engaging enough to dissuade him from his vision. Terah decided to unpack.

He may have thought he would stay for one night. One night became two. Two nights turned into three nights. Three nights stretched into a month. He kept telling his wife, "Listen, we are leaving soon. We will only be here for a week." A month later, his wife comes in with the realtor. "What is a realtor doing here? We are on our way to Canaan."

"No! We are just looking around to see what this place is like."

Don't Prolong Your Progress

God has spoken to you and told you what you need to do. Maybe the Lord said you need to get your education. But what happens if you go to work in the donut shop, just to save enough money to go back to college. Instead, the owner of the donut shop wants to make you a manager. He says, "Man! I see potential in you! Within two years, you could be a supervisor."

You only planned to stay for a month, but one month became two or three. All you wanted to do was save up a little money for college. You thought, *Wow! If I work a few extra hours, I could buy another car. I could get an apartment.* You worked extra shifts. A month became a year. A year became two or three years, and you forgot your lifetime goal. You did not plan to live in Haran. You planned to go to Canaan.

Now, you are married, and you have kids. *Well, I can't leave this job now and go to school.*

Your boss told you initially, "Don't worry. We have an education plan here. Once you work for three months, we will pay for your education."

You think, *Oh, yeah. Great!* But you didn't stay focused. You didn't have a mentor holding you accountable. You just camped in Haran when you intended to move to Canaan.

Don't spend one more night in Haran! God is saying, "It is time to get out of Haran. Get back on the road to Canaan." I don't know how much time elapsed between Genesis 11 and Genesis 12, but Terah ran out of time to transition.

> **GENESIS 11:32:**
>
> **32 And the days of Terah were two hundred and five years: and Terah died in Haran.**

Sometimes people say, "My father was in this business. My grandfather was in this business. My great-grandfather was in this business. My uncle was in this business. It is the only thing I know. Why change?" The fact that your father died there doesn't mean you have to die there as well.

PROCRASTINATION IS NOT PROGRESS!

The Lord began to speak to Abram. No matter how long you stay in Haran, Haran will never become Canaan. You could find a good preacher in Haran. They can "proph-a-lie" to you and do all kinds of stuff, but Haran will never become your Canaan.

You may stay at a job for many years because you are comfortable there. Often, God tells me how long I will be at a certain job before I go in. He is preparing me for my exit. You should always have an exit strategy. Believe me! They have one for you, in case things go wrong.

God informed me one morning, "Somebody, somewhere is planning your future. You'd better get your life in gear." Once that time comes, I begin to know when I have dwelt there for too long. It is time to move to the next thing. After a while, you get familiar. You get complacent.

I worked in a particular job for many years. I was used to my

DON'T UNPACK TOO EARLY

routine. I got there on Monday morning, and I had to go to meet Joe. "So, Joe! Tell me what you did from Friday until today." After that, I'd go to someone else's desk. I was checking here and checking there.

Then, in August 2016, God began to speak to me about a position that was several steps above my position. In the previous job, I wasn't supervising anyone. They were paying me a decent salary, but God had been stirring me up. "You need to change. This is not where you need to be."

God spoke to me about the story of the lepers who were sitting by the gate. They had to arise and make a move toward their advancement (2 Kings 7:3). I read about the new position online. The job was ten minutes from my house and paid significantly more than I was being paid.

There was much more responsibility. But, depending on the pay, I can handle a challenging work environment. That is why we have a local church! We go to church, and it sets us right. Then, we can return to deal with the responsibilities of our profession.

God has established you with victory in Christ Jesus, enabling you to handle anything in life. Your family is good, and you have a good church. Don't worry about your job. You won't have to spend the night there. You're going home at five o'clock. It doesn't matter if someone says, "Oh, don't take that job. That place is stressful." Listen! Just go in there and let the light of God shine.

I kept it to myself for months. One day, on my way to church, I mentioned it to my wife. "There is a position in that place. I have worked there before. This is how much it pays, but that place is demanding."

She said, "What do you mean? Tell me again how much they pay."

TRANSITION TO GREATER

She continued, "You've been complaining about your job. You know it is time for a change. Why don't you just find out about this other place?"

I had worked in the previous job for about eight years. For the first six years, I was a consultant. I didn't have the benefits. I had only been a full-time employee for two years. I thought, *If I stay here another eight years, I can get vested in the federal system. I don't want to leave now.*

One thing led to another. I went to church, and the brother leading pre-service prayer spoke some words that confirmed what was going on in me. I called the number right after the service and let them know I was interested in the position. I didn't want to wait until the next morning, because I knew I might change my mind.

By the next morning, they called me back as I was on my way to work. "We heard you were interested in the position." By that night, I was being interviewed for the job. It all just came together, and I decided to accept the position.

When I arrived for work, the place was chaotic. God began to give me wisdom. In my previous job, even though I asked God for wisdom, I didn't really think I needed it. Not much was going on. In the new place, I did not have a choice! I truly needed the wisdom of God. God helped, and the job became stable.

When things in that position were just settling into a routine, they came to me and asked, "If money was not an issue, what would be on your wish list? How would you change this program?"

When I first walked into the facility as a medical director, something came up in my spirit. I thought, *This place runs as an urgent-care facility, but it functions as a clinic.* So, I told them I would turn it into an urgent-care facility.

They said, "Hmmm. Urgent care? There is no other facility operating as an urgent-care facility for behavioral health." They conducted research and filed an application with the federal government for an urgent-care clinic.

In December 2018, I received a call from the VP. "Guess what? We just received a call from a senator congratulating us on having an urgent-care facility. They are awarding us four million dollars to build."

It is amongst the first in New York and God is putting us at the forefront of cutting-edge medicine and psychiatry in the city. We have to call different places to learn how. One of the things I realized is this: sometimes, you have to look at yourself the way others see you to really understand what God has put in you. This applies to those who see greater in you.

One day, my boss contacted me saying I needed to be at a meeting the next Monday at 8 a.m. I said, "Okay. Where is the meeting?" I didn't get a text back. I realized my boss wanted me to just be in the building. God helped me realize that people in the world look at the way I am described: "We have a triple-board-certified psychiatrist in addiction psychiatry, general psychiatry, and addiction medicine. He has extensive administrative experience to oversee this program."

They knew the potential of my qualifications. As long as they could get me into that building, they can put as many programs as they want around me. Because of the wisdom of God in me, none of those programs will fail. That is what God has done in positioning me there.

Every day, work is moving forward. At the time of this writing, they are building a primary-care suite, a pharmacy, and rooms for a substance-abuse program in the facility. They are putting urgent care

TRANSITION TO GREATER

in the facility, with an outpatient clinic of more than 1,500 patients. They say, "Just put Dr. Somorin there. That ship will not sink."

You need to get to the point where you are of such value to your employer that they are not afraid to throw anything at you. They know the ship will not sink because of the wisdom of God in you.

START WALKING TOWARD YOUR PROMISED LAND

You must walk towards your promise to receive the wisdom of God. God gives wisdom on demand.

There are two kinds of giants. When God tells you what you need to do, and you think of all the possible things that could go wrong, that is one set of giants. Once you have made a decision to possess your land of promise and walk towards it, you encounter other giants of opposition, face-to-face.

God has said that, whatever you face, no man shall be able to stand before you. God is committed to removing the giants in your path, not the ones next to your bed. God is not responsible for eliminating the ridiculous fears you have in your head. You must get beyond that and start walking towards your Promised Land.

Get out of Haran and start walking towards Canaan. Forget about how comfortable Haran is. Forget about the people you met there.

GENESIS 13:14-17

14 And the LORD said unto Abram, after that Lot was separated from him, Lift up now thine eyes, and look from the place where thou art northward, and southward, and eastward, and westward:

15 For all the land which thou seest, to thee will I give it, and to thy seed for ever.

16 And I will make thy seed as the dust of the earth: so that if a man can number the dust of the earth, then shall thy seed also be numbered.

17 Arise, walk through the land in the length of it and in the breadth of it; for I will give it unto thee.

God did not tell Abram to "look" until after Abram departed from Haran and separated from Lot. Some people have to separate from certain relationships because there are relationships that will hinder them from receiving further revelation from God. (I am not talking about your husband or wife!)

Why? The Lord knows that because of Bubba and Sally, those visions are dead on arrival. He knows you will call Sally first. "Sally, you won't believe this! God told me I should leave Haran and move towards Canaan. It is time to leave the donut shop."

Sally says, "You want to leave two weeks before you become Deputy Senior Temporary Manager? What kind of sense does that make? You've been waiting for this position for four years. The manager is on leave because of gout. His deputy is off work because of hypertension, and the supervisor is not able to get to work because of the bad weather. Now is the time for you to step into that temporary position. And, you are saying it is time to move?"

God knows that, until Sally agrees, you are not going anywhere. You will blab to everyone that you want to leave Haran and go to Canaan. But you know what their response will be.

"Who are you? Where did you hear about Canaan? Who in your family has been to Canaan? Who went beyond high school? At least you have your high school education. You have a secure job at the donut shop.

"You know the deputy manager's blood pressure was 200. If he keeps eating those donuts, he is going to have a stroke.

"Why are you making a move now? Just keep feeding him donuts! Keep pushing those jelly donuts. Before you know what is happening, the guy will be gone.

"You are comfortable now. Are you going to college and compete with younger people? It has been ten years since you left high school. Just be thankful. You are comfortable here."

Somewhere inside you, God is saying, "This is not it."

Don't Let Fear Hold You Back

Your boss doesn't know God's vision for your life. Wherever you are, you are meant to contribute. But never think your promotion has to be in that particular location. God is your source!

Some years ago, I established a substance abuse program. Some of the rules and regulations had changed, resulting in a decline in patient enrollment, and the program was no longer profitable. Because my program wasn't funded by the state, I had to use my own personal finances to supplement it. There was a point where things began to run dry, and I had to obtain a loan to pay salaries. I said, "If this continues, it is going to cause me to be bankrupt." I decided to shut it down.

Then, God began to speak to me. "You need to be open to different sources of income." (Many quotes that I put in my first book, *Seize Your Moment: Unmasking Everyday Opportunities*, came from that season.) An opportunity came to work for a weekend in another state.

God said, "Your victory is on the other side of your fear." If you are waiting for the fear to leave, you are not going to possess your Promised Land. You will stay in Haran.

When God says, "Position yourself," it is not just a physical positioning. It is a repositioning of your thinking. Change the way you think, and you will change where you are located. You may be in a place geographically, but mentally, you are in a position.

All the people who are there to hinder you are surrounding you. When God tells you to reposition yourself, you need to get yourself away from those people and surround yourself with people that will move you to your next level. That is what "repositioning yourself" means.

2 CORINTHIANS 1:20

20 For all the promises of God in him are yea, and in him Amen, unto the glory of God by us.

What do you do when you are presented with something that stretches your current level of thinking? You need to agree with God. God is seeking your agreement before He can do anything. Pastor Dean Brown says, "Some people are motivated, but they need to be activated." The purpose of this book is to activate you.

1 CORINTHIANS 2:9

9 But as it is written, Eye hath not seen, nor ear heard, neither have entered into the heart of man, the things which God hath prepared for them that love him.

If you wait until you are 100% sure, it will be too late. We must develop ourselves to the point where we immediately set ourselves in agreement with what the Spirit of God reveals. Even though there are questions in our minds, we must do it.

TRANSITION TO GREATER

Some people say they want a change, but they don't want to do anything differently. Make the change! Set yourself in agreement with God, change your position or mindset, and head towards the destination God has for you. Don't unpack before you get to your final destination. Stay on course.

Go back to what God initially said to you. At the end of each year, I go back and read my diary. I even go back and read old emails to see opportunities I may have missed. Take time to look at the vision God has given you. Make sure you haven't settled in the wrong place.

Don't look for a Canaan blessing while you are in Haran. The Canaan blessing is reserved for Canaan. If you are not there, you cannot experience it. You cannot have a Toyota serviced at a Jaguar dealership! If you want to experience the blessing of Canaan, you need to be in Canaan.

Don't be in the wrong place, wondering why the rain hasn't come. When you check the weather forecast, you must be specific about your location. God has a place of promise for you. Don't let anything stop you from possessing your Promised Land.

Chapter Three

Necessary Preparations

GOD WAITED FOR HIS PEOPLE TO MATURE so that they could possess the Promised Land. Often, we are waiting on God, but God is waiting for us. One of the examples from the Bible that I love is the story of the prodigal son. He wasted all of his money on riotous living, became poor, and joined himself to a stranger (Luke 15).

The prodigal son pleaded, "Listen, whatever you can spare to feed me..."

The man said, "Go and feed my pigs." The prodigal son went and began to feed the pigs.

One day, he thought, *What am I doing feeding pigs?* I don't know how long he fed the pigs. It could have been days, months, or years. Day one, he fed the pigs. Day two, he fed the pigs. Sunday, he fed the pigs. Monday, he fed the pigs. He woke up on Friday, looked around, and thought, *What am I doing among the pigs?*

The Bible says he came to himself (Luke 15:17). You need to come to yourself! There are times you come to yourself, and things just begin to happen. He came to himself and said, "Why am I sitting here amongst pigs? My father has servants. I know I have given up my sonship, but let me go back to my father and be a servant. I will do better than living amongst pigs."

He made that decision and took a step. He walked towards his father, and his father met and embraced him. The father was excited and put a robe on his son, celebrating him.

The Bible doesn't say an angel appeared to him. It doesn't say something spectacular happened. Instead, the Bible says he came to himself. He could have been around the pigs for so long, but his miracle was there at his father's house waiting for him.

The whole time he questioned, "God, don't You see my suffering? Haven't I suffered enough? I have been around these pigs so long that I even know their names," His miracle was there waiting at his father's house. He had to come to himself and then walk towards his miracle. He had to change where he was located and position himself in the right direction to get where he needed to be.

DON'T LIVE IN THE "DEFENSE" POSITION

There are keys to making the transition to greater. First, we need to live life from an offensive perspective, not the defensive position. In sports, the offensive strategies are designed to score or make progress on the field. The defensive plays are focused more on the opponent. Don't live life defensively.

ISAIAH 1:19

19 If ye be willing and obedient, ye shall eat the good of the land:

Often, we spend our time seeing how things cannot be done. Many become experts at this! Laziness will often reveal itself as fear.

PROVERBS 22:13

13 The slothful man saith, There is a lion without, I shall be slain in the streets.

The slothful man specifies that the lion is not ordinary but very fierce. Laziness is very precise when describing the opposition. "There is a fierce lion in the streets."

The Bible says if you bring seven people to a lazy man to explain why he should not be lazy, he will outwit all seven of them.

PROVERBS 26:16

16 The sluggard is wiser in his own conceit than seven men that can render a reason.

When God brings opportunity, is it laziness that prevents me from taking it, or is it fear? Or is it a lack of knowledge? If you bring seven men to talk to a lazy person, he will outwit all seven of them and give them perfect reasons why he should not get out of bed on a Monday morning.

"There is a job at McDonald's where you can get started."

"I've heard about that job at McDonald's, but I just finished attending a seminar at church. The word the Lord is telling me is that I should reach higher. I can't do anything other than something great! I need to step out into something great. That job is just too small for me."

"Do you want to go to school?"

"No, no. I am preparing myself for something really, really big. Once I see it, I will get that inner feeling." Right after he makes that statement, he will ask you for $10.00. "I need to try to get some lunch. I have been praying, and I want to break my fast. I can't break the fast because I have no money to eat."

We need to look for opportunities that allow God to increase us. If we do not act on ideas when they are fresh on our minds, they are going to be lost in the business of the day. Take a step back and see the opportunities that God is bringing your way.

Life cannot be lived by continually saying, "No." You need to say, "Yes." If you are going to move, you need to say, "Yes." Sometimes you need to say that "yes" and then believe God for the wisdom to carry it out. What God needs from you is that word, "Yes." Include more "yes" responses in your vocabulary.

STAY IN DRIVE!

Children are very innovative and imaginative. Their imagination is unlimited until they get older and settle into reality. But we can learn to maintain the power of our imagination to help us fulfill the plan of God.

You should never start your day in neutral. Some people are already done by noon because they started in neutral! Neutral is when you are thinking of your problem and your promise to the same extent.

It will take more than coffee and food to get you to God's destination. You need the blessings of God. You need an awareness of the blessings of God. You hear positive words from your pastor, but you hear negative words from the news. People on your job are telling you this is not going to work out.

For instance, we unveiled an electronic medical record system at the facility where I work. Everyone was worried and feeling as though the world was coming to an end. One of the doctors told me she was so flustered that a patient had offered to change seats with her! They asked me why I was so calm. One said, "I need some of what you have."

NECESSARY PREPARATIONS

I replied, "Don't worry. Just do what you can do. Take one day at a time." I looked as cool as a cucumber, at least on the outside.

Neutral is like half-and-half. You think half-problem and half-blessing. Reverse gear is when all you are thinking about is the problem. You are going backward. Drive is when the knowledge of the promise overwhelms the awareness of the problem. That is where we need to be. Stay in drive!

The current flows because there is a difference between one area and another. If you are going to move forward, something on the inside must be able to overwhelm what is going on outside.

Your face should not look like a thermometer. "Wow! I guess it is really bad out there today." You cannot afford to run your day in neutral. You must be in drive. You can't even get out of your driveway in neutral.

PSALM 119:92

92 Unless thy law had been my delights, I should then have perished in mine affliction.

PSALM 119:105

105 Thy word is a lamp unto my feet, and a light unto my path.

When you believe that the Word of God is a lamp unto your feet and a light unto your path, you know that you cannot go forward without it. You can only drive so far at night without turning on your headlights. Make sure the lamp of the Word of God is on so you can walk confidently. Sometimes we don't walk confidently because we know we are not walking in the light.

TRANSITION TO GREATER

We are hoping that by bumping into things, we can realize what we shouldn't be doing. We will just try to figure it out. If we don't bump into anything, thank God, we've made it through! When we bump into something, we say, "Uh-oh! Let me move a little bit to the left. If you wait for the light to be your path, you will be able to walk correctly.

It is essential to recognize that the Word of God is not a pit stop. It is not an added flavor, a topping. a sprinkle, or a seasoning. It is not a side dish; it is the main meal! Many times, people use the Word of God as a sprinkle. Someone may have worried all night. When it is time for them to go to work, they declare, "By the stripes of Jesus, I am healed." But it has no effect because they are words empty of power.

Make the Word the Main Dish

Like layers on a cake, the first layer is loaded with pure, unadulterated worry. The next layer is fear. The next layer is confusion mixed with depression. The topping is, "Though I walk through the valley of the shadow of death, I will fear no evil for Thou art with me."

People ask, "How is your day going?"

"Though I walk through the valley of the shadow of death, I will fear no evil for Thou art with me." That is a sprinkle, a topping! It is an added flavor. You cannot use the Word of God as a sprinkle.

You go to the restaurant and ask, "Can I have a Big Mac? Double the order and add the fries."

The attendant asks you, "What would you like to drink?"

You respond, "I'd like a diet Coke, please."

They say, "Would you like to supersize that?"

"No. I want a small, diet Coke."

The Word of God has to be the main meal. The Word of God has to be a way of life. The cake itself has to be made of the Word of God. Some cakes look so beautiful, but when you taste them, they are awful. "What did they put in it? Ugh! It is terrible."

The foundation of our lives has to be the Word of God. The Word can't just be the added flavor on top. It has to be the main meal. Put on your praise and speak what you believe.

Chapter Four

Live Loaded

PRAISE HAS NOTHING TO DO with your personality. It has everything to do with the opposition that we face and the position that is needed for victory. The Bible says we, as believers, are aware of the strategies and devices of the enemy. We can recognize who our enemy is and use the right warfare to fight him. The way to obtain victory is by meditating in our hearts and speaking out of our mouth. We need to start our day loaded!

Some people are too silent to walk in victory. Depression, anxiety, worry, and hopelessness are positions of life. Depression is a position. Anxiety is a position. Worry is a position. Hopelessness is a position.

Praise is a spiritual position that has nothing to do with personality. Some people think they have a non-praising personality. They think they do, but there is no such thing. "My personality is not a praise type. I just meditate on God's goodness. I let it sink in. I think about the goodness of the Lord." Some things will happen to try to steal the life, joy, and peace from our lives. Many things will attempt to put us in a bad attitude. To combat these things, we need to start our day loaded with the peace of God.

PSALM 68:19

19 Blessed be the Lord, who daily loadeth us with benefits, even the God of our salvation. Selah.

TRANSITION TO GREATER

You are loaded! Don't leave your loaded benefits at home. Instead, enter your day with your benefits in hand.

For example, when you get to work, the Human Resources department may tell you that something is not in line with your benefits. But if you have read your HR benefit policies from front to back, you know how many days off you are supposed to get. You know all the holidays. You know when a day is a floating or a sprinting holiday. If anyone tries to mess with your holiday, you take them to court.

We need to know the benefits of God and recognize that we are daily loaded with benefits. We are loaded! Don't live life just waiting to see what happens. Live life on the offensive, not on the defensive. Don't wait for sickness to come before you confess you are healed. That should be part of your confession list. There is a devil out there that is trying to take us out.

Don't wait until you hear there is a shooting before you cover your children with the blood. When you take them to school each day, apply the blood of Jesus on them. Prevention is better than cure.

That is a big part of what we do as Christians. You need to be in a mode of putting on your weapons. Put on the breastplate of righteousness and the shield of faith. Make sure your feet are shod with the preparation of the gospel of peace. Walk loaded with your benefits.

We need to live life on the offensive. No team wins just by having a strong defense; they must also have a good offense. You need to identify those things to which you are saying "yes."

How do we live life offensively? We meditate upon the promises of God.

#1 LOAD YOURSELF WITH THE PROMISES.

JOSHUA 1:8

8 This book of the law shall not depart out of thy mouth; but thou shalt meditate therein day and night, that thou mayest observe to do according to all that is written therein: for then thou shalt make thy way prosperous, and then thou shalt have good success.

Meditate knowing that you need God's Word as a light on your path. It is not optional. The Word of God should not depart out of your mouth. That is the point of this instruction. When you meditate day and night, you are not treating the Word of God as a sprinkle. It is not just something you say briefly in the morning.

God's Word should not depart. You meditate on it day and night. The Word is not just something you are trying; it is something you are living.

#2 CONFESS THE WORD OF GOD.

ROMANS 4:16-17

16 Therefore it is of faith, that it might be by grace; to the end the promise might be sure to all the seed; not to that only which is of the law, but to that also which is of the faith of Abraham; who is the father of us all,

17 (As it is written, I have made thee a father of many nations,) before him whom he believed, even God, who quickeneth the dead, and calleth those things which be not as though they were.

We need to be able to confess the Word of God over our situations, which is a vital part of living life offensively. We are not waiting for something terrible to happen. That is living from a defensive position. Some people run to church when something terrible happens. They are looking for a scripture. No! We live full of the Word!

Confess the Word over your life, your family, and your business. Don't wait for problems in your relationships to speak the Word over them. Speak the love of God in your home.

ISAIAH 60:18

18 Violence shall no more be heard in thy land, wasting nor destruction within thy borders; but thou shalt call thy walls Salvation, and thy gates Praise.

✳ ✳ ✳

DEUTERONOMY 11:21

21 That your days may be multiplied, and the days of your children, in the land which the Lord sware unto your fathers to give them, as the days of heaven upon the earth.

These verses describe your home! When you meditate on these truths until your heart and mouth are full of them, you will be confidently confessing the promise of God.

#3 LIVE IN AN ATMOSPHERE OF PRAISE.

PSALM 89:15-16

15 Blessed is the people that know the joyful sound: they shall walk, O Lord, in the light of thy countenance.

16 In thy name shall they rejoice all the day.

If you know the joyful sound, you will walk in the light of the countenance of God with God's favor and blessing saturating your life.

PSALM 89:15-16 MSG

15 Blessed are the people who know the passwords of praise, who shout on parade in the bright presence of God.

16 Delighted, they dance all day long; they know who you are, what you do—they can't keep it quiet!

Blessed are the people who know the passwords of praise! Praise opens the door to the supernatural. When we are full of joy about His promises, we can't keep our praise quiet.

Praise is the password! Knowing the password of praise helps you to live life offensively. You can experience God's presence, regardless of the situation.

The Bible says we enter into His presence with thanksgiving and enter His courts with praise (Psalm 100:4). Thank God now for the password of praise! No matter what you are going through, there is a password that gets you into the presence of God.

#4 CHOOSE TO SEE THE GREATER.

You must choose to see greater. Nobody can see it for you. You cannot transition to what you cannot see. You must be able to see beyond your current circumstances. You need to be able to live a life of expectation. Believe in a better future.

God spoke to me a few years ago and said, "If your eyesight and your vision are the same things, there is a problem." Your eyesight and your vision should not be the same thing. You should be able to see beyond where you are.

TRANSITION TO GREATER

You can have perfect vision and still be blind. I am not just talking about something spiritual, but about the natural realm also. The eye is not really how you see. The eye is what allows the information to enter, but how you see is a function of the brain. If someone had a lesion in the occipital lobe, that person would be blind even though their eyes are perfect. If there is nothing anatomically wrong with their eyes, if something were to happen in the occipital lobe, they would not be able to interpret what is coming through their eyes. They would be effectually blind.

It is essential to be able to see beyond the situation you are currently experiencing. My pastor, Pastor Dean Brown, shared a message many years ago entitled, *This Is Not What I Have Seen*. In it, he explained, you need to be at that place you have seen in your spirit. To arrive at that place, you must cast a vision. That is what a vision board does. You need to have something in your heart that says, "Coming Soon." You need some kind of a billboard within telling you this is not the end. Something is coming soon.

LIFT UP NOW THINE EYES

Abram lived with his father. We don't know about his relationship with God before God told him to come out of his father's house. After he departed from his father's house, God led him.

> **GENESIS 12:4-5**
>
> **4 So Abram departed, as the Lord had spoken unto him; and Lot went with him: and Abram was seventy and five years old when he departed out of Haran.**
>
> **5 And Abram took Sarai his wife, and Lot his brother's son, and all their substance that they had gathered, and the souls that**

they had gotten in Haran; and they went forth to go into the land of Canaan; and into the land of Canaan they came.

The Bible says Abram, Sarai, and Lot went to the land of Canaan. Abram built an altar and traveled to Egypt because of the famine. Then, he came back.

GENESIS 13:14-18:

14 And the Lord said unto Abram, after that Lot was separated from him, Lift up now thine eyes, and look from the place where thou art northward, and southward, and eastward, and westward:

15 For all the land which thou seest, to thee will I give it, and to thy seed [descendants] for ever.

16 And I will make thy seed as the dust of the earth: so that if a man can number the dust of the earth, then shall thy seed also be numbered.

17 Arise, walk through the land in the length of it and in the breadth of it; for I will give it unto thee.

18 Then Abram removed his tent, and came and dwelt in the plain of Mamre, which is in Hebron, and built there an altar unto the Lord.

God brought Abram out of his familiar environment, away from his family. God had to wait for Lot to leave before He showed him the land. God said, "Look." Why didn't God tell him to look while he was in his father's house or while Lot was still with him?

Sometimes God moves you out of a situation, away from certain people, and then tells you to look. There may be times that you must be separated from people who will hinder you from experiencing what God has in store for you.

God won't always explain why He is doing certain things. We need

TRANSITION TO GREATER

to just act in obedience. Now that we see what happened, we can see the pattern and obtain wisdom from it. God brought Abram out of his familiar environment, away from his family, apart from his nephew and instructed Abram, "Look." My question for you is: "What has, your focus?" You cannot be looking at the right thing and be heading in the wrong direction.

> **GENESIS 13:14-18 AMP**
>
> **14** The Lord said to Abram, after Lot had left him, "Now lift up your eyes and look from the place where you are standing, northward and southward and eastward and westward;
>
> **15** for all the land which you see I will give to you and to your descendants forever.
>
> **16** I will make your descendants [as numerous] as the dust of the earth, so that if a man could count the [grains of] dust of the earth, then your descendants could also be counted.
>
> **17** Arise, walk (make a thorough reconnaissance) around in the land, through its length and its width, for I will give it to you."
>
> **18** Then Abram broke camp and moved his tent, and came and settled by the [grove of the great] terebinths (oak trees) of Mamre [the Amorite], which are in Hebron, and there he built an altar to [honor] the Lord.

The first thing God says is: "Look!" Too many people are looking at what has been set before them. Instead, they could choose their focus and set it before their eyes. You decide what will have your focus! Then, set it before you and maintain your focus.

This is one thing God had to accomplish in Abram to help him to transition to greater. Abram was only acquainted with the things associated with his father's house. God created in Abram the capacity to increase by causing him to look beyond his circumstances and focus on something else. Rather than giving Abram a vague picture, God instructed him, "Look towards the stars." God will always give us a direction in which to look. In the instruction, we will discover the correct path to take.

We must be purposeful in our focus. We don't have to physically be in the Promised Land to picture the Promised Land. We can imagine the Promised Land while we are in the wilderness.

The Bible says, *"Where there is no revelation (or vision), people cast off restraint"* (Prov. 29:18 NIV). The reason God shows us where we are going is to help us identify when we have arrived. By establishing this in advance, God ensures that we will not settle in the wrong place, wander in the wilderness, or live an aimless life.

If we are going to transition to greater, we must see greater. Instead of giving our focus to the things which surround us, we must purposefully place before our eyes what the Lord has revealed or instructed.

HEBREWS 11:1-3

1 Now faith is the substance of things hoped for, the evidence of things not seen.

2 For by it the elders obtained a good report.

3 Through faith we understand that the worlds were framed by the word of God, so that things which are seen were not made of things which do appear.

If you are going to transition to greater, you must be able to receive direction from God. You must also be able to receive the inner pictures that the Lord desires to form in your inner man. What you see in your heart and what is visible in front of you are two different things.

TRANSITION TO GREATER
2 CORINTHIANS 5:7

7 For we walk by faith, not by sight.

Have you ever experienced a time when someone stood in front of you, trying to get your attention? Why were they trying to get your attention? Although they were standing in front of you, you were not looking at them. What you see is what your mind has chosen as the object of its focus. You need to see greater to experience greater.

You can be in a bad neighborhood and set your eyes on the right thing. Meditating on the right thing will change your zip code. You can be in a good neighborhood and set your mind on the wrong thing. It is not your neighborhood. It is your focus! Casting vision does not cost anything, but it will save you from so much.

Whether as an individual or as a couple, you need to be able to see greater. For instance, my wife and I were talking about investments and where we want to see ourselves in a few years. We challenged ourselves concerning the next year to set a goal for something. Initially, the goal sounded really ridiculous. Then, I began to meditate on it. I said, "You know what? If we do this and we cut out a few things, this goal is possible." I became excited when I began to focus on the goal!

If we don't have a vision and a goal for our money, we will just be spending here and spending there. We will cast off restraint and not be focused. When we focus on something, we will be amazed at all we can accomplish.

You are not too poor until you are too poor to dream! Everybody is moving in response to something they have seen. Some people have seen status-quo or failure, while others have seen progress. Some people are reliving the past or experiencing uncertainty.

If God cannot change your focus, He cannot cause you to inherit the promise. There was a reason the Lord sent the spies into the Promised Land. He wanted to create a proper picture. They returned with the wrong image, and the Lord called it "an evil report."

When God sent you to spy into your future, and He gave you a glimpse of it, what kind of report did you bring back? You must lift up your eyes. Psalm 121:1 says, *"I will lift up mine eyes unto the hills, from whence cometh my help."*

Stop positioning yourself at "eye-level" to your situation. You are seated far above. Look from your current position in Christ without worrying about where you are, where you hoped you would be by now, and where you think you are supposed to be. Just look from where you are.

Forget about the biological clock, the financial clock, or whatever detail has kept your attention. Look from where you are.

"Arise, walk through the land [you see] in the length of it and in the breadth of it; for I will give it unto thee" (Gen. 13:17). What do you see? Do you see yourself graduating? Do you imagine yourself owning your own business? Do you picture yourself being with someone who treats you well? Do you see yourself out of debt? Happy? Joyful? Can you imagine being a blessing in the house of God and in His kingdom or enjoying life with a wonderful family?

Your Promised Land is limited by your vision. Stop looking at just anything. Set the right thing in front of your eyes.

To go to the next level, people need to see differently. Some people are wholly occupying their Promised Land right now because that is all they have seen. There are bosses, boyfriends, girlfriends, family members, corporations, credit card companies, lending institutions, and payday loan sharks who hope they will not see differently!

These institutions hope people will continue behaving the same way financially, emotionally, relationally, etc.

Some people are waiting until their pastor finally gets the right word to deliver them, but they have not done anything differently. They are hoping that word will come this year since it didn't come last year or the year before last. They are waiting, but they haven't changed any behavior.

Some people depend on the fact that we do not change what we see. The minute we shift our focus, we will move. It is instant! We see another vision, and BOOM! We are gone. Where we are right now is not the issue. The issue is, what are we seeing?

GENESIS 13:16

16 And I will make thy seed as the dust of the earth: so that if a man can number the dust of the earth, then shall thy seed also be numbered.

God is interested in more than just helping us pay off credit card debt. God is interested in generational wealth. We need to get beyond just living for today. Stop living just for today because God's plan is for generational wealth.

GENESIS 13:17

17 Arise, walk through the land in the length of it and in the breadth of it; for I will give it unto thee.

Arise and walk through the land. Is that an impossible task? No. All Abram had to do was get up and walk. There are certain things God will instruct you to do to provide vision.

MAKE A THOROUGH RECONNAISSANCE IN THE LAND.

Perhaps, you are believing God to be able to move to a particular neighborhood. You need to perform a reconnaissance mission. Go and spy out that neighborhood. Take a drive and look at some good houses. Go on a reconnaissance mission!

You need to look. Are you believing God to be able to go to college? Go and look at some different colleges. Get your vision going! Are you believing God to work in a certain company? Go in there and see the place for yourself. Go to some open houses. Perform a reconnaissance mission. That will help you see and imagine the land.

Arise and walk through the land, through its full length and width. You need to know precisely where God is taking you. When He gives you that vision, you need to go on that reconnaissance mission. That will help to set it before your eyes. Hang around some healthy marriages. Do reconnaissance around some healthy marriages and healthy families.

The extent of your obedience is the limit of your possession. Arise. Walk in the land through its length and width. Abram had never possessed any of it yet, but this requirement created in him the capacity. He was looking up. He was looking northward, southward, and eastward. He was looking at the skies and at the stars. He was looking at the sand.

God will give you a focus. You need to do the possible if you expect God to do the impossible. These are not things that cost any money but will create capacity. The four points I have shared will help to build the capacity for the increase and greatness. They are things you have to do in obedience to God that will help you to see greater.

TRANSITION TO GREATER

#1 Load yourself with the Promises of God.

#2 Confess the Word of God.

#3 Live in an atmosphere of praise.

#4 Choose to see the greater.

Look at the principles God taught Abram. If you follow those principles, you will reap what God has ordained for you. Things are being deposited in you for the years to come. Possess the Promised Land God has in store for you and believe God to be somewhere else by next year. Perform some reconnaissance missions. Expand that which God has in store. Choose what you are looking at and stop looking at your circumstance. It is time to look towards heaven, which is the origin of your help.

Chapter Five
Take the Next Steps

GOD WILL GIVE YOU AN INSTRUCTION to obey. If you are obedient, further guidance will come. After Lot separated from Abram, God showed Abram the Promised Land (Gen. 13:14-15).

Simply start. Don't wait for conditions to be perfect. Don't wait for things to happen. If you are going to transition to greater, there are times you must simply start something. Take the next step. The Lord told Abram to arise and walk through the land.

JAMES 2:26

6 For as the body without the spirit is dead, so faith without works is dead also.

You may be exercising your faith to believe God for a house or for a new church building. You may want to go to a particular college. God wants you to go there and just walk around the place. God needed to expand Abram's capacity to receive, so He told him to walk through the land.

Some people are already in their Promised Land. They already possess all they have the capacity to possess. When you talk about the Promised Land, they wonder what you are saying. As we have already learned, Abram's father was heading to Canaan, but something happened in Haran. He felt comfortable. Maybe he said, "Why bother with Canaan? This place is good enough."

It is possible to live in the "land of Good Enough" and never attain what God has in store for us. But the promise is in Canaan. There is a place of promise where God expects you to be "operating on all cylinders."

God once asked me, "On how many cylinders are you operating?"

I thought, *Cylinders? I don't know how many cylinders I have.*

God said, "You have six, but you are only operating on one. If you expect the full blessing, but you are only operating on one cylinder, that means there are five other cylinders on which I expect you to operate."

Many believers are overwhelmed because they are only operating on one cylinder. We cannot find them in the church because they have a nine-to-five job and need the whole weekend to recuperate. They don't think they can attend church on Sunday. How can God help them if they are not in His presence or submitted to His Word?

An Increased Level of Wisdom

When we begin to move to the place of promise, we see there is an increased level of wisdom needed.

There is a story about a man who would go fishing, catch a fish, and then throw it back. He would catch another fish and keep it. They asked him why he was throwing some of the fish back. He said, "Well, my frying pan is a particular size. If I catch a fish that is too big, it

TAKE THE NEXT STEPS

won't fit into my frying pan. I have to throw the big ones back and wait until I catch fish that will fit into my frying pan."

That seems funny, but many people apply this concept in their daily lives. Somebody provides an opportunity, and the first thing they consider is the size of their frying pan. When somebody presents an idea, it passes through a filter of limiting questions. That is why God had to increase Abram's capacity to receive.

God said, "I am going to give you this land."

Abram lived in Haran and was comfortable there. Maybe he was head of the library board and the school board. They knew him. His Facebook page had all the likes. For God to cause Abram to inherit Canaan, God had to increase his capacity.

I received another revelation from the installation of a new electronic health record system at the facility where I work. Many of the other doctors I work with were losing their composure, trying to adapt to the new system. It reminded me of the children of Israel, who, while in Egypt, complained about Egypt. But as they began to walk toward the Promised Land, they began to see the changes and asked, "Why did you bring us out here to die? Just take us right back."

As soon as we began training for the new system, I made a statement to the doctors. "Over the next couple of weeks, you will look back at the previous medical record system and say, 'I love that record system so much! It was the best thing since sliced bread.'" That is precisely what happened! When they brought the new system, I felt like the choir was singing "What a Friend We Had in the Old System."

The minute something new comes up, you may think, *Oh, no! I love the previous way. It wasn't that bad.*

God had to prepare Abram. Perhaps he said, "When I begin to

TRANSITION TO GREATER

prepare you for new opportunities, I don't want your mind to revert back to that 12-inch frying pan." God knew that it would take a process. He told him to lift up his eyes, so he did not look at what happening around him. He would look above at the God Who was his source.

Teddy Roosevelt said, "Do what you can with what you have and where you are."[1]

Ken Keyes Jr. says, "To be upset over what you don't have is to waste what you do have."[2]

John Mason said, "People with enterprise accomplish more than others because they go ahead and do it before they are ready."[3]

When I look at the person who supervises the area where I work, I look at the way they respond. The way administrators respond is very different from the way doctors respond. Many doctors never get into administration. Doctors and administrators think in a completely different way. We feel like everything has to be lined up before we take the next step. In administration, they say, "Opportunity has come. Go with it. Everything will come together. Just move."

If you ask the doctors, "Who is ready for a new electronic health record system?" Nobody will say they are ready. Just set the date and do it. Whatever you need to do to get ready, get it done. Stay up all night if necessary. Move forward. People complained and yelled, but we just had to go with it. Sometimes people do things because demand is placed on them. If you are going to experience God's goodness, you have to learn how to place a demand upon yourself. You know how quickly you can get something done when your boss says it is due by a specific date. When was the last time you gave yourself a due date?

When it comes to your own vision, you like to crawl. When it

TAKE THE NEXT STEPS

comes to someone else's vision, you are prepared to take a leap. You have been putting up goals for the year. All you do is change the year at the top of the page each January. You may add a few things to it each time. One year, you want to be better at something. The next year, you put down "much better." Then, it is "really, really greater." When it comes to goals people set for you at work, you may sound very positive. "Come on! Let's get this done." Use that same boldness for what God has shown you. Use it to write your book!

Chapter Six

Surrounded by Surmountable Opportunities

ONE VITAL TRUTH THE LORD SPOKE TO ME is that we are surrounded by surmountable opportunities. As a believer, these opportunities are surmountable. Don't stop believing in opportunities. Very often, the difference between extraordinary and ordinary is "extra." Find your little extra!

ECCLESIASTES 11:1-6

1 Cast thy bread upon the waters: for thou shalt find it after many days.

2 Give a portion to seven, and also to eight; for thou knowest not what evil shall be upon the earth.

3 If the clouds be full of rain, they empty themselves upon the earth: and if the tree fall toward the south, or toward the north, in the place where the tree falleth, there it shall be.

4 He that observeth the wind shall not sow; and he that regardeth the clouds shall not reap.

5 As thou knowest not what is the way of the spirit, nor how the bones do grow in the womb of her that is with child: even so thou knowest not the works of God who maketh all.

6 In the morning sow thy seed, and in the evening withhold not thine hand: for thou knowest not whether shall prosper, either this or that, or whether they both shall be alike good.

Sometimes we are just one audience short of a breakthrough. The Bible says we should cast our bread upon the waters and give a serving to seven and also to eight. This passage is talking about sowing and reaping. As you have opportunities to sow, to invest, and to be a blessing, take them. Invest your skills and your time into the kingdom.

Sometimes God wants you to position yourself and develop your skills above what you are already doing because He knows there is an evil coming. There is a shift coming. Your favorite boss, who has told you that you have a job for life, could leave. Evil can be upon the earth. That is why you should keep your skills sharp.

You should constantly be monitoring and developing your skills in the industry where you function. See yourself as a corporation instead of just an employee. Look at yourself as an asset to the company where you work. Constantly monitor your value.

I am always monitoring what I have to offer. As a psychiatrist, I realize that not all psychiatrists have an interest in administration or finances. The same thing I offer in my present position could be worth so much more in a different area.

Improvements that Create Opportunity

Little things begin to distinguish you from other people because they create opportunities for you.

SURMOUNTABLE OPPORTUNITIES

PROVERBS 18:16

16 A man's gift maketh room for him, and bringeth him before great men.

Many times, people spend their time around average people because they are not using their gifts. When you are using your gifts, people don't have to like you. Your gift makes room for you, creating an entrance that is not contestable.

The Bible says, *"He that observes the wind shall not sow; and he that regards the clouds shall not reap"* (Eccl. 11:4). There are times you need to be sowing. Maybe you need to go to school, take an extra job for a season, or build on a skill that you have been neglecting.

There is never a perfect time to do something extra. You can always find a reason to keep things the way they are. This is status-quo. Why do you have to do anything extra? You may be happy just coming into the church and relaxing. Why do you need to extend yourself? You may know you could be of value to the ministry in one area or another, but you keep it hidden.

God wants you to step out. He that observes the wind shall not sow; and he that regards the clouds shall not reap. Not only does this indicate there is a time to sow, but it also reveals there is a season to reap.

You don't determine the location of your harvest. When you see God as your source, you are going to come to the conclusion that there are two basic limitations: how much we believe and our capacity to receive from God.

CREATE CAPACITY FOR INCREASE

Firstly, God's power is limited by how much we believe. The

TRANSITION TO GREATER

Bible says that with God, nothing shall be impossible. (Luke 1:37) In Ephesians 3:20, it says God is able to do exceedingly abundantly above all we ask according to the power that works in us.

The other limitation can be our container. For example, in 2 Kings 4:1-7, the Bible talks about how Elisha saw a woman whose husband had died. Creditors were coming to take her two sons. He asked what he could do for her, and he asked, "What do you have in your house?"

She said, "All I have is a little jar of oil."

He said, "Go and borrow vessels, not a few." She borrowed them, and Elisha told her to pour out the oil. She began to pour until the first vessel was full. She called for another container, and another, and another. She kept pouring until the last container was full. The Bible says that at that point, the oil ceased.

God wants us to open up or prepare some more vessels. If you are going to transition to greater, you must create capacity for the increase, which occurs as we create vessels to retain what the Lord wants to deposit.

What are vessels? They are investment opportunities. They are opportunities for you to use your giftings in a different location. Sometimes it is the same gift; you are just exposing it to a different audience.

For instance, my books have exposed me to a different audience, whether it is in Canada, New York, Florida, Texas, or Nigeria. The messages in the books have opened doors for me to teach men's workshops in places I have never been before, to new audiences! That is part of how you create capacity. How many containers do you have?

Elisha told the widow to borrow vessels from all her neighbors and told her not to gather just a few. "Don't gather a few. We need

SURMOUNTABLE OPPORTUNITIES

to create capacity." The creditors were coming to get her sons, and she had nothing. By that one opportunity, she was able to pay all her creditors and live on what was left.

Be obedient to what God is saying to you. The provision arrived because she was obedient to collect the vessels. What if she had refused to do it? "No, no! I don't want to borrow people's vessels."

The man of God asked her, "What do you have in your house?" She had oil, and the prophet told her to pour it. Do something with what you have!

He didn't tell her to go and get her neighbor's oil. You have the oil, but you need containers. What gift has God given you? Build up yourself so you can present your gift to different people, not just to people of your ethnic origin, gender, zip code, or to your church family and friends. Move out of your comfort zone and use the same gift in a different area. What do you have in your house?

Whatever God has for you is going to stretch you. A man's gift makes room for him and will bring him before kings (Pro. 18:16). Give to seven and also to eight (Ecc. 11:2). The Bible says when the enemy comes one way, he will flee seven ways (Deut. 28:7).

Some years ago, I was running a substance abuse program in addition to working another job. The program closed because it wasn't viable financially. Patients weren't coming in, and I didn't have another stream of finances to help me weather the shortfall. I ended up borrowing money from the bank. With the interest and overhead, I decided I couldn't keep borrowing and chose to end the program.

A couple of years later, God began to open my eyes, showing me that the program didn't have to end. The problem was that I didn't have enough streams of income. Every business may experience a rough patch. I had not prepared for it by arranging to have other streams of income. I should have saved money for a business emergency.

I connected those two scriptures about giving a portion to seven and also to eight and about the enemy fleeing seven ways. I began to believe God for seven sources of income. Now, as much as I get excited about one business, I do not lose sight of income from other areas. I keep myself open to opportunities. I never say to myself, "Oh, this is it! I am going to let go of everything else."

That is one reason I don't allow myself to be involved in office politics. That job is just one of seven. If I am bogged down by one, how will I manage the other six? I do what I have to do and move to the next responsibility.

In that situation, God opened some doors for me to bring in extra money to pay off the bank. I received a call about an opportunity in South Carolina. I went there for three weekends, and the amount they paid me wiped out the debt. I wasn't sure about going, so I prayed about it. When I finished praying, I looked up and saw the bills. That is when God told me, "Your victory is on the other side of your fear." I took the plunge, accepted the job, and paid off the bank.

I am still doing that job today. Why? I am not going to close that door. I can invest that money. I didn't say, "Well, I paid the bank, and I don't need that job anymore." No. I went through the process of getting licensed in South Carolina. Every couple of months, they call and ask me to come down. They fly me in for a weekend, and I come back home in time for church on Sunday. If God opens a door, don't close it!

SURMOUNTABLE OPPORTUNITIES
BE WILLING TO WORK HARDER

Next, you must be willing to work harder. As you can see, none of these opportunities came by me just taking it easy.

ECCLESIASTES 10:18-19

18 By much slothfulness the building decays; and through idleness of the hands the house drops through [leaks].

19 A feast is made for laughter, and wine makes merry: but money answers all things.

I was meditating on that scripture when I looked up and saw that something was leaking in my house. It was during a time when money was tight. I thought *Hmmm. I wonder how much the plumber will charge for this?* The solution was not a prayer; the answer was hard work. Through idleness of the hands, the house leaks. If your house is leaking, work harder.

I say things that sound like clichés, but I have lived and am still living by them. When opportunities come to me, fear shows up too. God began to show me through the scriptures that laziness manifests itself as fear.

God blesses what we put our hands to do. Opportunity often involves you working harder than you are now. Many people have a view that their yoke is supposed to be easy, and their burden is supposed to be light (Matt. 11:30).

PROVERBS 6:6-11

6 Go to the ant, thou sluggard; consider her ways, and be wise:

7 Which having no guide, overseer, or ruler,

8 Provideth her meat in the summer, and gathereth her food in the harvest.

> **9** How long wilt thou sleep, O sluggard? when wilt thou arise out of thy sleep?
>
> **10** Yet a little sleep, a little slumber, a little folding of the hands to sleep:
>
> **11** So shall thy poverty come as one that travelleth [a prowler], and thy want [need] as an armed man.

When you wake up, and your bed is surrounded by bills, you might as well be surrounded by armed men. If you are lazy, you will miss opportunities God is bringing your way.

The opportunity will present itself as something that places a demand on you and limits your time for TV or social media. It may involve you studying longer and harder. It may mean enrolling in a course, taking an extra job, or doing an internship. Someone said, "I can't do an internship because I won't get paid." At least you are working, and that work may open opportunities for you.

> **PROVERBS 26:13 NKJV**
>
> **13** The lazy man says, "There is a lion in the road! A fierce lion is in the streets!"

That is exactly what I said about the opportunity in South Carolina. A lion! Get behind me, Satan! There is something about laziness. Laziness helps you to define the fear clearly. It gives you 20/20 vision. The lazy man doesn't just say there is a lion in the road. The lazy man says it is a fierce lion in the streets. Yes! It will kill him dead. If you take this job, they will kill you. You might as well go ahead and write your will.

After they called the lazy man and told him about the job, and he has turned it down because it is too demanding, he hangs up and turns over on his bed.

SURMOUNTABLE OPPORTUNITIES

PROVERBS 26:14

14 As the door turns upon his hinges, so doth the slothful upon his bed.

He describes how fierce the lion is, hangs up the phone, and gets into a more comfortable position in bed. He wants to go back to his dream.

PROVERBS 26:15

15 The slothful hides his hand in his bosom [or in the bowl]; it grieves him to bring it again to his mouth.

He puts his hand in the bowl and says, "Oh, no! Not today. I need help to get this into my mouth." While he is still trying to do it, another call comes in. Seven people from church are calling to motivate him. He has an excuse for each one of them as to why he can't do anything.

PROVERBS 26:16

16 The sluggard is wiser in his own conceit than seven men that can render a reason [answer sensibly].

Some people are very intelligent, but they are very lazy! They outwit seven men who can answer sensibly. If you are going to transition to greater, you must be willing to work harder.

STOP SETTLING FOR REALITY. CHANGE IT!

In 2 Corinthians 5:7, the Bible says we walk by faith and not by sight. Your Heavenly Father was not willing to leave reality the way it was, so He created heaven and earth. He placed the same creative gene on the inside of you. What are you going to create? What are you going to subdue?

Calvin Coolidge said, "We do not need more things that are seen; we need more things that are unseen."[4]

E. W. Howe says, "People are always neglecting something they can do in trying to do something they cannot do."[5]

Someone may say, "I have decided to go to medical school."

You might respond, "That's powerful. Have you completed high school?

"No, but I believe this is where God is leading me."

It is when we play it safe that we create a world of utmost insecurity. We don't tap the resources of God until we attempt the impossible.

Francois de La Rochefoucauld said, "Mediocre minds usually dismiss anything as impossible that reaches beyond their own understanding."[6]

Someone said, "Even a coward can praise God, but it takes a person of courage to follow Him."[7]

Godly Vision Involves Risk

There is always a risk. Don't wait for fear to leave and don't focus on the negatives. Don't focus on how fierce the lion is. Focus on what God has spoken to you. Focus on the pros, and you manage the risks.

A dream that does not involve risk is not really worth being called a dream. If you never take risks, you will never accomplish great things. There is always a risk. Otherwise, there would not be a need for faith. Remember, your victory is on the other side of your fear.

The children of Israel were afraid of going into the Promised

SURMOUNTABLE OPPORTUNITIES

Land. But God does not change your Promised Land to accommodate your fear. He waits for you to grow up, maturing beyond the fear, and develop sufficient faith to possess your Promised Land. The Lord is not going to tolerate your fears. He knows you have heard the Word so you cannot plead ignorance anymore.

Stop waiting on God to bring your Promised Land to you. The land doesn't move. You have to move into it and possess it. You have to be built up. God has faith in you that you can be built up to possess it. The degree of faith God has in you is based on what He knows you have been hearing. If you've been attending a church under a pastor feeding you the Word of God, God knows your potential.

If your vision doesn't intimidate you, then you are officially in a rut. You need to have a "Coming Soon" mentality. Place a note somewhere for yourself to see in the morning and get excited. Don't wait for events to get you excited. Be excited by the vision for which you are reaching.

Motivate yourself. What have you written on the "Coming Soon" billboard of your heart? Does it excite you? Does it make you want to jump out of bed, or does it make you want to hit the snooze button? Does it make you want to work harder? Does it keep you motivated, inspired, and reaching for greater heights?

"We don't need more intellectual power. We need more spiritual power. He who does not dare will not get his share. Look for ways to flex your "risk muscle." Keep it in proper shape by experimenting and trying new things. People who take risks are people you will lose against if you don't take risks. You must be willing to take risks."[8]

2 TIMOTHY 1:7

7 For God hath not given us the spirit of fear; but of power, and of love, and of a sound mind.

TRANSITION TO GREATER

Fear is one thing that will try to keep us away from the promises and keep our territory limited. Fear's primary objective is to constrict our territory. On the other hand, the goal of faith is to enlarge our territory.

When you dare for nothing, you hope for nothing. God wants us to bite off more than we can chew and to live by faith, not by sight. Dream big and say, "Yes!" to God's plan for your life. Focus on what God has said and not on what is dead.

Pastor Dean Brown said, "Faith is doing things regardless of the consequences." You must choose to see greater. Don't hesitate to use corresponding actions. There are things you need to start doing right now. Don't hesitate to walk toward your promise.

Refuse to settle in Haran. If you have settled in Haran, it is time to repack. If you have unpacked at the wrong place, get yourself back together and start walking towards your Promised Land.

Dream Big.

Think Big.

Act Big.

Pray Big.

Receive Big.

Chapter Seven

Breakthrough in the Midst of Adversity

LET'S TALK ABOUT BREAKTHROUGH in the midst of adversity. What do you do when God puts your breakthrough at a time and place right next to your trial?

The breakthrough may be in the midst of your pain, your famine, your sorrow, your confusion, or your financial difficulty. You may be desperate, perplexed, or disillusioned. Sometimes adversity is there to signal that your breakthrough is about to happen. A woman is pregnant for nine months, and then she goes into labor. At the time of her most significant pain comes the greatest blessing. She is focused on birth, so she is willing to go through the pain.

Sometimes, during the time of your greatest pain is when the greatest blessing is manifested.

> **2 KINGS 6:24-33, 7:1-20 (NKJV)**
>
> **24 And it happened after this that Ben-Hadad king of Syria gathered all his army, and went up and besieged Samaria.**
>
> **25 And there was a great famine in Samaria; and indeed they besieged it until a donkey's head was sold for eighty shekels**

of silver, and one-fourth of a kab of dove droppings for five shekels of silver.

26 Then, as the king of Israel was passing by on the wall, a woman cried out to him, saying, "Help, my lord, O king!"

27 And he said, "If the Lord does not help you, where can I find help for you? From the threshing floor or from the winepress?"

28 Then the king said to her, "What is troubling you?" And she answered, "This woman said to me, 'Give your son, that we may eat him today, and we will eat my son tomorrow.'

29 So we boiled my son, and ate him. And I said to her on the next day, 'Give your son, that we may eat him'; but she has hidden her son."

30 Now it happened, when the king heard the words of the woman, that he tore his clothes; and as he passed by on the wall, the people looked, and there underneath he had sackcloth on his body.

31 Then he said, "God do so to me and more also, if the head of Elisha the son of Shaphat remains on him today!"

32 But Elisha was sitting in his house, and the elders were sitting with him. And the king sent a man ahead of him, but before the messenger came to him, he said to the elders, "Do you see how this son of a murderer has sent someone to take away my head? Look, when the messenger comes, shut the door, and hold him fast at the door. Is not the sound of his master's feet behind him?"

33 And while he was still talking with them, there was the messenger, coming down to him; and then the king said, "Surely this calamity is from the Lord; why should I wait for the Lord any longer?"

***

BREAKTHROUGH IN THE MIDST OF ADVERSITY
2 KINGS 7:1-20 (NKJV)

1 Then Elisha said, "Hear the word of the Lord. Thus says the Lord: 'Tomorrow about this time a [a]seah of fine flour shall be sold for a shekel, and two seahs of barley for a shekel, at the gate of Samaria.' "

2 So an officer on whose hand the king leaned answered the man of God and said, "Look, if the Lord would make windows in heaven, could this thing be?" And he said, "In fact, you shall see it with your eyes, but you shall not eat of it."

3 Now there were four leprous men at the entrance of the gate; and they said to one another, "Why are we sitting here until we die?

4 If we say, 'We will enter the city,' the famine is in the city, and we shall die there. And if we sit here, we die also. Now therefore, come, let us surrender to the army of the Syrians. If they keep us alive, we shall live; and if they kill us, we shall only die."

5 And they rose at twilight to go to the camp of the Syrians; and when they had come to the outskirts of the Syrian camp, to their surprise no one was there.

6 For the Lord had caused the army of the Syrians to hear the noise of chariots and the noise of horses—the noise of a great army; so they said to one another, "Look, the king of Israel has hired against us the kings of the Hittites and the kings of the Egyptians to attack us!"

7 Therefore they arose and fled at twilight, and left the camp intact—their tents, their horses, and their donkeys—and they fled for their lives.

8 And when these lepers came to the outskirts of the camp, they went into one tent and ate and drank, and carried from it silver and gold and clothing, and went and hid them; then they came back and entered another tent, and carried some from there also, and went and hid it.

TRANSITION TO GREATER

9 Then they said to one another, "We are not doing right. This day is a day of good news, and we remain silent. If we wait until morning light, some punishment will come upon us. Now therefore, come, let us go and tell the king's household."

10 So they went and called to the gatekeepers of the city, and told them, saying, "We went to the Syrian camp, and surprisingly no one was there, not a human sound—only horses and donkeys tied, and the tents intact."

11 And the gatekeepers called out, and they told it to the king's household inside.

12 So the king arose in the night and said to his servants, "Let me now tell you what the Syrians have done to us. They know that we are hungry; therefore they have gone out of the camp to hide themselves in the field, saying, 'When they come out of the city, we shall catch them alive, and get into the city.' "

13 And one of his servants answered and said, "Please, let several men take five of the remaining horses which are left in the city. Look, they may either become like all the multitude of Israel that are left in it; or indeed, I say, they may become like all the multitude of Israel left from those who are consumed; so let us send them and see."

14 Therefore they took two chariots with horses; and the king sent them in the direction of the Syrian army, saying, "Go and see."

15 And they went after them to the Jordan; and indeed all the road was full of garments and weapons which the Syrians had thrown away in their haste. So the messengers returned and told the king.

16 Then the people went out and plundered the tents of the Syrians. So a seah of fine flour was sold for a shekel, and two seahs of barley for a shekel, according to the word of the Lord.

17 Now the king had appointed the officer on whose hand he leaned to have charge of the gate. But the people trampled

him in the gate, and he died, just as the man of God had said, who spoke when the king came down to him.

18 So it happened just as the man of God had spoken to the king, saying, "Two seahs of barley for a shekel, and a seah of fine flour for a shekel, shall be sold tomorrow about this time in the gate of Samaria."

19 Then that officer had answered the man of God, and said, "Now look, if the Lord would make windows in heaven, could such a thing be?" And he had said, "In fact, you shall see it with your eyes, but you shall not eat of it."

20 And so it happened to him, for the people trampled him in the gate, and he died.

This story provides us with a biblical example of the breakthrough appearing in the middle of difficult adversity. The Word of the Lord came and said, "...tomorrow about this time." How do you go from boiling children on one day to seeing a complete economic change? They experienced a 180-degree turnaround!

Our text in Second Kings 7:3 says, *"Now there were four leprous men at the entrance of the gate; and they said to one another, 'Why are we sitting here until we die?'"*

These leprous men were forced to live on the outskirts of the city. They were sitting at the gate, waiting for a change in the situation. They said, "Listen, people are boiling their children in the city. If we stay here, we know for sure we are going to die because there is no surplus of food to feed us. If we go to the camp of the Syrians, we have two options. They could either keep us or kill us. If they kill us, we are going to die anyway. Let's walk towards the possibility of life."

You may think, *What does this have to do with me?* How often do you stay in a place, hoping something will happen? You have been there so long, and things have not changed. You know it is time to make a change, but you are too afraid to step out and do what God is asking you to do. You know what will happen if you go back. That place may be filled with death, but it is a familiar place. You decide not to go forward; you choose to go back.

The woman goes back to the guy who treats her like trash. Once a year, he buys her a card on Valentine's Day to say, "I love you." She goes back to that relationship, that place, and that lifestyle because she is afraid to take a step into something God has for her.

The lepers said, "Going back is not an option. Staying here is not an option." Many of us look back and think *I don't want to go back. I don't want to go forward. I will just stay here.* We don't make a decision to stay. We just fail to make a decision to move. You didn't say "yes" to the proposal. So, that is a "no." How often do we stay in the same place, hoping something will happen? Are you in a financial or emotional state that has no life? It is time to cross over to your breakthrough.

They rose at twilight (2 Kings. 7:5). That is significant. The Bible doesn't say an angel came at twilight or something meaningful happened to motivate them. They assessed their situation, looked at where they were, and said, "We have to do something different."

At twilight, they arose and began to walk towards the possibility of life. As they walked, the Lord caused the Syrian army to hear the sounds of chariots, of horses, and of a great army (2 Kings 7:6). The soldiers said to one another, "Look, the king of Israel has hired against us the kings of the Hittites and the kings of the Egyptians to attack us!"

Therefore, they arose and fled at twilight and left the camp intact (2 Kings 7). When did the Syrians flee? At twilight, as soon as the lepers began to take steps towards the army of the Syrians, God multiplied

BREAKTHROUGH IN THE MIDST OF ADVERSITY

the sound of their footsteps. The Syrians were hearing the sounds of a great army, not just the sounds of three lepers. The minute you assess your situation and begin to take a step towards your destiny, God starts to multiply the sound of your steps in the ears of your enemies.

God did not multiply anything while they were sitting at the gate. As they began to walk towards the possibility of life, the power of God began to move. Faith without works is dead (James 2:20). Something is about to change! Refuse to stay in the same position year in and year out. Choose to walk towards your promise. God began to multiply the sound as they walked toward the camp.

Their breakthrough was right next door! In the city, there was hunger and desperation. Right down the road, there was abundance. Your breakthrough will always be within your reach. Always! God will never put your breakthrough beyond your reach.

What steps do you need to take to transition from famine to a place of abundance? How long have you been at that gate wondering when the scarcity is going to end?

How many children have to be boiled, so to speak? How bad do things have to be? You will come to a point when you have to leave the gate. You may say, "It can't be worse than this."

Someone has said, "When your chances are slim to none, go with slim." I want to list some valuable lessons from this story:

LESSON #1

Never allow fear to stop you from making a decision to improve your life.

TRANSITION TO GREATER

Any decision of value will have a risk attached to it. Angels didn't appear to the lepers. They were probably the least educated and definitely in the worst position to make a change. They had not heard, to the best of our knowledge, the word from Elisha. They simply evaluated their situation and made a decision. Sometimes you need to look around you and say, "I can do better than this."

LESSON #2

Never Be So Overwhelmed by Negative Circumstances that You Stop Looking for Opportunities for Your Breakthrough.

Your breakthrough can be right there amid your adversity.

JAMES 1:2-8

2 My brethren, count it all joy when you fall into various trials,

3 knowing that the testing of your faith produces patience.

4 But let patience have its perfect work, that you may be perfect and complete, lacking nothing.

5 If any of you lacks wisdom, let him ask of God, who gives to all liberally and without reproach, and it will be given to him.

6 But let him ask in faith, with no doubting, for he who doubts is like a wave of the sea driven and tossed by the wind.

7 For let not that man suppose that he will receive anything from the Lord;

8 he is a double-minded man, unstable in all his ways.

BREAKTHROUGH IN THE MIDST OF ADVERSITY

Ask God for wisdom when you are going through a trial. The lepers operated in this wisdom. They looked and said, "This is what is going on; this is what is here. Why sit here until we die?"

I previously mentioned the new electronic medical record system put into operation in the facility where I work. That was a big transition! A month later, we opened one of the first behavioral health urgent care facilities in New York State. It operates seven days a week, 365 days a year.

We had two major transitions, one after the other, I commented to some of the other doctors, "These are the changes we are making, and we've had to get rid of some bugs in the system." They were upset about the bugs in the system!

I told them about the opportunities for the urgent care facility. There were weekend hours available for those who wanted to work. I thought they would jump at the chance to work. Maybe some of them needed extra money to pay off student loans.

Instead, the opportunity flew over their heads! All they thought about was fixing the electronic medical record system. They couldn't get beyond the issue.

I thought, *We are operating something that has the potential to change lives. The facility is for children as well as adults. This is ground-breaking. There is nothing like it anywhere!*

But they were only consumed with the problems. The only thing they wanted to know was how the issues would affect them. They wanted to fix the electronic medical record system before they thought about anything else.

Sometimes you can be so consumed with one thing that you miss what God is doing. You may be overwhelmed with what your boss is doing. A moment of opportunity can come, but you are so distracted by the little things that you do not see the bigger picture.

People are coming to take tours of our new facility, which is staffed with social workers, nurses, and doctors. Nobody has done anything like it. We applied for a grant and received it, and everyone wants to know how we did it.

In the midst of what you consider the most difficult time, God can open your eyes to a breakthrough.

LESSON #3

Never Be So Consumed with the Problem that You Miss Your Word of Deliverance

There was a word of deliverance that came in 2 Kings 7:1. *"Then Elisha said, Hear ye the word of the Lord; Thus saith the Lord, Tomorrow about this time shall a measure of fine flour be sold for a shekel, and two measures of barley for a shekel, in the gate of Samaria."*

Notice what the Bible says in Daniel 2:21-22:

DANIEL 2:21-22 (NKJV)

21 And He changes the times and the seasons; He removes kings and raises up kings; He gives wisdom to the wise And knowledge to those who have understanding.

22 He reveals deep and secret things; He knows what is in the darkness, And light dwells with Him.

God can change your season, and He can do it in twenty-four hours! God is able to change seasons and times. It could be sunny one minute, and the next minute it could be pouring rain like nobody's business!

The Lord removes kings and raises up kings. The boss who has been there for so long can be moved to another location, or the boss who caused your blood pressure medication to be changed three times may leave. Stop adjusting your blood pressure meds simply because of a certain individual. If God says that something will change in 24 hours, believe it. Don't allow yourself to become part of your circumstances. Stay responsive to God.

Don't let the fabric of adverse conditions become part of who you are. If you do, you will not respond to God correctly. You are a child of the Creator, not a victim of circumstance. You and your situation should never be on the same level.

No matter how bad the situation is, your ears should always be open to the Word of the Lord and not to the circumstance. The solution will come from inside you.

PROVERBS 20:27

27 The spirit of man is the candle of the Lord, searching all the inward parts of the belly.

They may call you to say there is an emergency, and you must rush somewhere. No matter how hurried you are, you must still find your car keys. No one would say, "This is such an emergency. I am just going to run." Where is the wisdom in that? No matter how bad the emergency is, you must still find your car keys.

In the same way, the Word of the Lord is where salvation originates. No matter how bad the situation is, you must keep your spirit open to your word of deliverance. You don't need to understand every detail of how it will be accomplished: you just need to believe.

TRANSITION TO GREATER
LESSON #4

If the Word of God comes to you with a timeframe, believe it.

Do not mock it, whether it makes sense to you or not. Be in the camp of the believers, not the doubters. Even if it doesn't come with a timeframe, you should always believe that today could be the day that thing changes.

The king leaned on his right-hand man, while the Word of the Lord was coming. The man in whom he trusted said, "If God would make windows in heaven and rain things down, how could this thing be?" The Bible said he would see it with his eyes, but he would not eat it.

Why did this man say those things? Consider these three factors:

1. The intensity of the famine
2. The severity of the famine
3. The duration of the famine

How often do we allow the intensity, severity, and duration of our trial to make us lose sight of what God is saying? When the trial started, were you excited about what God was doing? Did you come to church with expectations? After six months, after seven months, after a year, things changed. After two years of believing, "Oh, man!" After three years, you didn't think it was going to happen. You began to look for another way. The intensity! The severity! The duration! "It has been going on for so long. Why does God wait until it seems things are so bad?"

BREAKTHROUGH IN THE MIDST OF ADVERSITY

To experience a turnaround in the famine, this man reasoned it would have to be gradual. Even if the Syrians moved out, they would take all their belongings with them. Things would have returned to normal gradually.

God caused them to go from famine to abundance in twenty-four hours! Every time you wake up, say, "This is the day the Lord has made. Things can change in twenty-four hours!"

Your situation may have been going on for 10, 15, or 20 years, but as long as you hold onto the Word of God, it does not have to take that long for the situation to turn around. The question is, are you going to see and partake of the victory, or are you going to see it and not eat of it? Change is coming!

On what side of the change will you be? During the difficulty, people may be present who will sympathize with you. But when the word comes that something is about to change, they may not rejoice with you. Some people are sympathizers, and some people are rejoicers. Few people are both!

You don't need a sympathizer when the word about deliverance comes. "Twenty-four hours! Get packed. We are getting out of here! I'm not going to call Sally. I know who I am going to call. I need a praiser when that word comes."

I don't need someone to say, "Twenty-four hours? This thing has been going on for ten years. The doctor has had you on this medication for fifteen years. Ever since I've known you, you've had cancer."

God says, "Within twenty-four hours, something is about to change." The man thought that if things were going to change, it would be gradual. There would be time to adjust. If the Word of God tells you things are about to change in twenty-four hours, they will!

TRANSITION TO GREATER
GENESIS 17:19-21 (NKJV)

19 Then God said: "No, Sarah your wife shall bear you a son, and you shall call his name Isaac; I will establish My covenant with him for an everlasting covenant, and with his descendants after him.

20 And as for Ishmael, I have heard you. Behold, I have blessed him, and will make him fruitful, and will multiply him exceedingly. He shall beget twelve princes, and I will make him a great nation.

21 But My covenant I will establish with Isaac, whom Sarah shall bear to you at this set time next year."

Someone may say, "I know you have anxiety and have been going to the doctor three times a week. When God begins to heal you, maybe you can reduce that to two visits a week. After six months, you will go once a week. Then, you will go every other week because tt will be gradual."

God quickened in my spirit that His Word can act as an accelerant. An accelerant is something that speeds up a process. How many people need an accelerant? It took fifteen years to get into that problem. You don't have another fifteen years to come out of it. You need an accelerant to speed up the process! God's Word is an accelerant to the progress that will move you into your Promised Land.

Always be ready for your life to get better. Never allow anyone to tell you it must come in phases. Sometimes it does, and other times it is expedited. God can move you from the back to the front in one swoop. He can cause your healing to be expedited. Do they say the recovery time is six months? He can make it in six days.

Live a life of expectation, no matter what is going on around you. You may have imagined your breakthrough would come one way. You have tried seven different things. Try the eighth way! Never disconnect from the Word of the Lord. That is where your breakthrough originates. Take your eyes off the intensity, the severity, and the duration of the problem. Focus on the Word of the Lord.

LESSON #5

One Decision Can Change Your Life Forever

The lepers made a decision to walk toward their promise.

JAMES 2:26

26 For as the body without the spirit is dead, so faith without works is dead also.

To what do you need to add works or actions today? Which corresponding actions do you need to add to your faith to trigger something to move in the right direction? One decision! The lepers assessed the situation, made a decision, and took action.

What action will cause you to cross from the gate of famine to the place of plenty? You can move from the place of sickness to the place of healing. You can progress from a place of lack to a place of abundance. You can go from the place of depression to the place of joy. You can vacate the place of insufficiency and move into the land of more than enough. You can go from the place of pain to the place of walking in the fullness of joy.

They assessed the situation. They did not wait for God to evaluate it for them. They made a decision by asking, "Why sit here until we die?" They didn't stop there. They did the most important thing: they took action.

TRANSITION TO GREATER
They Crossed Over to the Possibility of Life

You can't get the job if you don't apply for it. You can't get into college if you don't enroll. Certain things won't happen unless you act because they require corresponding actions.

Never consider adversity as a permanent situation. Never! Make the decision that you are not going to die there. You are going through and coming out in victory on the other side! God has given you the victory.

1 CORINTHIANS 10:13

13 No temptation has overtaken you except such as is common to man; but God is faithful, who will not allow you to be tempted beyond what you are able, but with the temptation will also make the way of escape, that you may be able to bear it.

Be constantly scanning your environment for your way of escape. Where is your escape? You are coming out of this! Within twenty-four hours, something can change. Declare the Word of God over your life!

BREAKTHROUGH IN THE MIDST OF ADVERSITY
ENDNOTES

1   Mason, John "Conquering an Enemy Called Average." Insight International, Tulsa, OK 1996

2   "Ken Keyes Jr.." AZQuotes.com. Wind and Fly LTD, 2019. https://www.azquotes.com/quote/352347

3   Mason, John "Conquering an Enemy Called Average." Insight International, Tulsa, OK 1996

4   Calvin Coolidge, "The Things That Are Unseen." Wheaton College, Norton, Massachusetts, June 19, 1923

5   E. W. Howe Quotes." BrainyQuote.com. BrainyMedia Inc, 2019. https://www.brainyquote.com/quotes/e_w_howe_163171

6   "Francois de La Rochefoucauld Quotes." BrainyQuote.com. BrainyMedia Inc, 2019. https://www.brainyquote.com/quotes/francois_de_la_rochefouca_137121

7   Anonymous, Sermon Index.net, http://www.sermonindex.net/modules/articles/index.php?view=article&aid=30572

8   Mason, John "Conquering an Enemy Called Average." Insight International, Tulsa, OK 1996

A Prayer for Salvation

Father, thank You for sending Your Son, Jesus Christ, to die for me on the cross. I believe in my heart that Jesus is the Son of God, that He died on the cross, and that He rose again from the dead. I confess that He is my Lord and Savior. I commit my life to You; come into my life and be my Lord and Savior.

In Jesus' name,

Amen

About the Author

'Lanre Somorin MD is a board-certified psychiatrist and has been practicing since 1995. He is also an associate pastor. He has a specialty in Addiction Psychiatry.

Somorin's mission is to help people discover hope and to live purposeful lives. Somorin is the medical director for an outpatient mental health facility with seven clinical sites.

He has been listed in the Top Doctors' issue of the Hudson Valley (NY) Magazine yearly since 2006. He owned and operated an outpatient substance abuse rehab facility and has held various leadership positions, including clinical consultant to the Army Substance Abuse Clinic in West Point, NY. He has a private behavioral health practice in Monroe, NY. He is married and is the father of two.

Also by Author

SEIZE YOUR MOMENT

In *Seize Your Moment, Unmasking Everyday Opportunities*, board-certified psychiatrist and associate pastor 'Lanre Somorin, MD, reveals thirty-one keys to overcoming the barriers that prevent us from capitalizing on what daily life has to offer. Combining scripture with practical tools, motivational quotes, and insightful advice, Somorin empowers readers to take full control of their lives.

Starting with the vital role preparation plays in identifying and taking advantage of opportunities, Somorin explores the need for understanding and wisdom, tips for dealing with adversity, and the importance of removing distractions. You'll discover how the simplest ideas often represent opportunity and recognize that successfully capitalizing on opportunity does not mean avoiding hard work.

www.seizeyourmomentnow.com

Also by Author

THE POWER OF A NEW BEGINNING

Roadblocks and set backs don't have the final say in your life!

There is power in a new beginning to transition you into an area that is greater in scope, greater in fulfillment, and greater in resources. The ability to transition into this new beginning is available to you.

Associate Pastor and Board Certified Psychiatrist, 'Lanre Somorin, M.D., reveals important truths about the adversities that stand in the way of transition into greater, identifying these hindrances and explaining how to overcome them.

The Power of a New Beginning is a book designed to enable you to firmly grasp your destiny and transition into the greater that God has established for you. Step into your new beginning today!

For More Information

contact

www.seizeyourmomentnow.com

Made in the USA
Middletown, DE
26 April 2022